Poems in English

Poems In English

by

Samuel Beckett

GROVE PRESS, INC.   NEW YORK

Library of Congress Catalog Card Number: 63-11076
Sixth Printing

Acknowledgments: *Whoroscope* was first
published by Nancy Cunard, The Hours
Press, 1930; *Echo's Bones*, published by
George Reavey, Europa Press, 1935.

Manufactured in the United States of America

DISTRIBUTED BY RANDOM HOUSE, INC., NEW YORK

GROVE PRESS, INC., 53 EAST 11TH STREET,
NEW YORK, NEW YORK 10003

Poems in English

Other Works by Samuel Beckett

Published by Grove Press

Endgame
Happy Days
Krapp's Last Tape
   and Other Dramatic Pieces
Malone Dies
Molloy
Murphy
Proust
The Unnamable
Waiting for Godot
Watt
Molloy / Malone Dies / The Unnamable
   (*in one volume*)

Contents

I Whoroscope

What's that?
An egg?
By the brothers Boot it stinks fresh.
Give it to Gillot.

Galileo how are you
and his consecutive thirds!
The vile old Copernican lead-swinging son of a
    sutler!
We're moving he said we're off—Porca
    Madonna!
the way a boatswain would be, or a sack-of-
    potatoey charging Pretender.
That's not moving, that's *moving*.   10

What's that?
A little green fry or a mushroomy one?
Two lashed ovaries with prostisciutto?
How long did she womb it, the feathery one?
Three days and four nights?
Give it to Gillot.

Faulhaber, Beeckman and Peter the Red,
come now in the cloudy avalanche or Gassendi's
    sun-red crystally cloud

(11)

and I'll pebble you all your hen-and-a-half ones
or I'll pebble a lens under the quilt in the midst
        of day.   20

To think he was my own brother, Peter the
        Bruiser,
and not a syllogism out of him
no more than if Pa were still in it.
Hey! pass over those coppers,
sweet millèd sweat of my burning liver!
Them were the days I sat in the hot-cupboard
        throwing Jesuits out of the skylight.

Who's that? Hals?
Let him wait.

My squinty doaty!
I hid and you sook.   30
And Francine my precious fruit of a house-and-
        parlour foetus!
What an exfoliation!
Her little grey flayed epidermis and scarlet
        tonsils!
My one child
scourged by a fever to stagnant murky blood—
blood!
Oh Harvey belovèd
how shall the red and white, the many in the
        few,

(dear bloodswirling Harvey)
eddy through that cracked beater?   40
And the fourth Henry came to the crypt of the
      arrow.

What's that?
How long?
Sit on it.

A wind of evil flung my despair of ease
against the sharp spires of the one
lady:
not once or twice but . . . .
(Kip of Christ hatch it!)
in one sun's drowning   50
(Jesuitasters please copy).
So on with the silk hose over the knitted, and
      the morbid leather—
what am I saying! the gentle canvas—
and away to Ancona on the bright Adriatic,
and farewell for a space to the yellow key of
      the Rosicrucians.
They don't know what the master of them that
      do did,
that the nose is touched by the kiss of all foul
      and sweet air,
and the drums, and the throne of the fæcal
      inlet,
and the eyes by its zig-zags.
So we drink Him and eat Him   60

and the watery Beaune and the stale cubes of
          Hovis
because He can jig
as near or as far from His Jigging Self
and as sad or lively as the chalice or the tray asks.
How's that, Antonio?

In the name of Bacon will you chicken me up
          that egg.
Shall I swallow cave-phantoms?

Anna Maria!
She reads Moses and says her love is crucified.
Leider! Leider! she bloomed and withered,   70
a pale abusive parakeet in a mainstreet window.

No I believe every word of it I assure you.
Fallor, ergo sum!
The coy old frôleur!
He tolle'd and legge'd
and he buttoned on his redemptorist waistcoat.
No matter, let it pass.
I'm a bold boy I know
so I'm not my son
(even if I were a concierge)   80
nor Joachim my father's
but the chip of a perfect block that's neither old
          nor new,
the lonely petal of a great high bright rose.

(14)

Are you ripe at last,
my slim pale double-breasted turd?
How rich she smells,
this abortion of a fledgling!
I will eat it with a fish fork.
White and yolk and feathers.
Then I will rise and move moving   90
toward Rahab of the snows,
the murdering matinal pope-confessed amazon,
Christina the ripper.
Oh Weulles spare the blood of a Frank
who has climbed the bitter steps,
(René du Perron . . . . !)
and grant me my second
starless inscrutable hour.

1930

Notes

René Descartes, Seigneur du Perron, liked his ome-
lette made of eggs hatched from eight to ten days;
shorter or longer under the hen and the result, he says,
is disgusting.

He kept his own birthday to himself so that no astrologer could cast his nativity.
The shuttle of a ripening egg combs the warp of his days.

P. 11, l.   3   In 1640 the brothers Boot refuted Aristotle in Dublin.

4   Descartes passed on the easier problems in analytical geometry to his valet Gillot.

5-10   Refer to his contempt for Galileo Jr., (whom he confused with the more musical Galileo Sr.), and to his expedient sophistry concerning the movement of the earth.

17   He solved problems submitted by these mathematicians.

P. 12, l. 21-26   The attempt at swindling on the part of his elder brother Pierre de la Bretaillière—The money he received as a soldier.

27   Franz Hals.

29-30   As a child he played with a little cross-eyed girl.

31-35   His daughter died of scarlet fever at the age of six.

37-40 Honoured Harvey for his discovery of the circulation of the blood, but would not admit that he had explained the motion of the heart.

P. 13, l. 41 The heart of Henri iv was received at the Jesuit college of La Flèche while Descartes was still a student there.

45-53 His visions and pilgrimage to Loretto.

56-65 His Eucharistic sophistry, in reply to the Jansenist Antoine Arnauld, who challenged him to reconcile his doctrine of matter with the doctrine of transubstantiation.

P. 14, l. 68 Schurmann, the Dutch blue-stocking, a pious pupil of Voët, the adversary of Descartes.

73-76 Saint Augustine has a revelation in the shrubbery and reads Saint Paul.

77-83 He proves God by exhaustion.

P. 15, l. 91-93 Christina, queen of Sweden. At Stockholm, in November, she required Descartes, who had remained in bed till midday all his life, to be with her at five o'clock in the morning.

94 Weulles, a Peripatetic Dutch physician at the Swedish court, and an enemy of Descartes.

(17)

II Echo's Bones

The Vulture

dragging his hunger through the sky
of my skull shell of sky and earth

stooping to the prone who must
soon take up their life and walk

mocked by a tissue that may not serve
till hunger earth and sky be offal

Enueg I

Exeo in a spasm
tired of my darling's red sputum
from the Portobello Private Nursing Home
its secret things
and toil to the crest of the surge of the steep
        perilous bridge
and lapse down blankly under the scream of the
        hoarding
round the bright stiff banner of the hoarding
into a black west
throttled with clouds.

Above the mansions the algum-trees
the mountains
my skull sullenly
clot of anger
skewered aloft strangled in the cang of the wind
bites like a dog against its chastisement.

I trundle along rapidly now on my ruined feet
flush with the livid canal;
at Parnell Bridge a dying barge
carrying a cargo of nails and timber

rocks itself softly in the foaming cloister of the
        lock;
on the far bank a gang of down and outs would
        seem to be mending a beam.

Then for miles only wind
and the weals creeping alongside on the water
and the world opening up to the south
across a travesty of champaign to the mountains
and the stillborn evening turning a filthy green
manuring the night fungus
and the mind annulled
wrecked in wind.

I splashed past a little wearish old man,
Democritus,
scuttling along between a crutch and a stick,
his stump caught up horribly, like a claw, under
        his breech,
smoking.
Then because a field on the left went up in a
        sudden blaze
of shouting and urgent whistling and scarlet
        and blue ganzies
I stopped and climbed the bank to see the game.
A child fidgeting at the gate called up:
"Would we be let in Mister?"
"Certainly" I said "you would."
But, afraid, he set off down the road.
"Well" I called after him "why wouldn't you
        go on in?"

(23)

"Oh" he said, knowingly,
"I was in that field before and I got put out."
So on,
derelict,
as from a bush of gorse on fire in the mountain
            after dark,
or, in Sumatra, the jungle hymen,
the still flagrant rafflesia.

Next:
a lamentable family of grey verminous hens,
perishing out in the sunk field,
trembling, half asleep, against the closed door
            of a shed,
with no means of roosting.
The great mushy toadstool,
green-black,
oozing up after me,
soaking up the tattered sky like an ink of
            pestilence,
in my skull the wind going fetid,
the water . . .

Next:
on the hill down from the Fox and Geese into
            Chapelizod
a small malevolent goat, exiled on the road,
remotely pucking the gate of his field;
the Isolde Stores a great perturbation of sweaty
            heroes,
in their Sunday best,

come hastening down for a pint of nepenthe or
        moly or half and half
from watching the hurlers above in Kilmain-
        ham.

Blotches of doomed yellow in the pit of the
        Liffey;
the fingers of the ladders hooked over the
        parapet,
soliciting;
a slush of vigilant gulls in the grey spew of the
        sewer.

Ah the banner
the banner of meat bleeding
on the silk of the seas and the arctic flowers
that do not exist.

Enueg II

world world world world
and the face grave
cloud against the evening

de morituris nihil nisi

and the face crumbling shyly
too late to darken the sky
blushing away into the evening
shuddering away like a gaffe

veronica mundi
veronica munda
give us a wipe for the love of Jesus

sweating like Judas
tired of dying
tired of policemen
feet in marmalade
perspiring profusely
heart in marmalade
smoke more fruit
the old heart the old heart
breaking outside congress

doch I assure thee
lying on O'Connell Bridge
goggling at the tulips of the evening
the green tulips
shining round the corner like an anthrax
shining on Guinness's barges

the overtone the face
too late to brighten the sky
doch doch I assure thee

Alba

before morning you shall be here
and Dante and the Logos and all strata and
                mysteries
and the branded moon
beyond the white plane of music
that you shall establish here before morning

                grave suave singing silk
                stoop to the black firmament of areca
                rain on the bamboos flower of smoke
                    alley of willows

who though you stoop with fingers of com-
                passion
to endorse the dust
shall not add to your bounty
whose beauty shall be a sheet before me
a statement of itself drawn across the tempest
                of emblems
so that there is no sun and no unveiling
and no host
only I and then the sheet
and bulk dead

Dortmunder

In the magic the Homer dusk
past the red spire of sanctuary
I null she royal hulk
hasten to the violet lamp to the thin K'in music
           of the bawd.
She stands before me in the bright stall
sustaining the jade splinters
the scarred signaculum of purity quiet
the eyes the eyes black till the plagal east
shall resolve the long night phrase.
Then, as a scroll, folded,
and the glory of her dissolution enlarged
in me, Habbakuk, mard of all sinners.
Schopenhauer is dead, the bawd
puts her lute away.

Sanies I

all the livelong way this day of sweet showers
        from Portrane on the seashore
Donabate sad swans of Turvey Swords
pounding along in three ratios like a sonata
like a Ritter with pommelled scrotum atra cura
        on the step
Botticelli from the fork down pestling the
        transmission
tires bleeding voiding zeep the highway
all heaven in the sphincter
the sphincter

müüüüüüüüde now
potwalloping now through the promenaders
this trusty all-steel this super-real
bound for home like a good boy
where I was born with a pop with the green of
        the larches
ah to be back in the caul now with no trusts
no fingers no spoilt love
belting along in the meantime clutching the
        bike
the billows of the nubile the cere wrack
pot-valiant caulless waisted in rags hatless
for mamma papa chicken and ham

(30)

warm Grave too say the word
happy days snap the stem shed a tear
this day Spy Wedsday seven pentades past
oh the larches the pain drawn like a cork
the glans he took the day off up hill and down
          dale
with a ponderous fawn from the Liverpool
          London and Globe
back the shadows lengthen the sycomores are
          sobbing
to roly-poly oh to me a spanking boy
buckets of fizz childbed is thirsty work
for the midwife he is gory
for the proud parent he washes down a gob of
          gladness
for footsore Achates also he pants his pleasure
sparkling beestings for me
tired now hair ebbing gums ebbing ebbing
          home
good as gold now in the prime after a brief
          prodigality
yea and suave
suave urbane beyond good and evil
biding my time without rancour you may take
          your oath
distraught half-crooked courting the sneers of
          these fauns these smart nymphs
clipped like a pederast as to one trouser-end
sucking in my bloated lantern behind a Wild
          Woodbine

cinched to death in a filthy slicker
flinging the proud Swift forward breasting the
                   swell of Stürmers
I see main verb at last
her whom alone in the accusative
I have dismounted to love
gliding towards me dauntless nautch-girl on the
                   face of the waters
dauntless daughter of desires in the old black
                   and flamingo
get along with you now take the six the seven
                   the eight or the little single-decker
take a bus for all I care walk cadge a lift
home to the cob of your web in Holles Street
and let the tiger go on smiling
in our hearts that funds ways home

Sanies II

there was a happy land
the American Bar
in Rue Mouffetard
there were red eggs there
I have a dirty I say henorrhoids
coming from the bath
the steam the delight the sherbet
the chagrin of the old skinnymalinks
slouching happy body
loose in my stinking old suit
sailing slouching up to Puvis the gauntlet of
        tulips
lash lash me with yaller tulips I will let down
my stinking old trousers
my love she sewed up the pockets alive the live-
        oh she did she said that was better
spotless then within the brown rags gliding
frescoward free up the fjord of dyed eggs and
        thongbells
I disappear don't you know into the local
the mackerel are at billiards there they are
        crying the scores
the Barfrau makes a big impression with her
        mighty bottom

Dante and blissful Beatrice are there
prior to Vita Nuova
the balls splash no luck comrade
Gracieuse is there Belle-Belle down the drain
booted Percinet with his cobalt jowl
they are necking gobble-gobble
suck is not suck that alters
lo Alighieri has got off au revoir to all that
I break down quite in a titter of despite
hark
upon the saloon a terrible hush
a shiver convulses Madame de la Motte
it courses it peals down her collops
the great bottom foams into stillness
quick quick the cavaletto supplejacks for
                    mumbo-jumbo
vivas puellas mortui incurrrrrsant boves
oh subito subito ere she recover the cang
                    bamboo for bastinado
a bitter moon fessade à la mode
oh Becky spare me I have done thee no wrong
                    spare me damn thee
spare me good Becky
call off thine adders Becky I will compensate
                    thee in full
Lord have mercy upon us
Christ have mercy upon us

Lord have mercy upon us

Serena I

without the grand old British Museum
Thales and the Aretino
on the bosom of the Regent's Park the phlox
crackles under the thunder
scarlet beauty in our world dead fish adrift
all things full of gods
pressed down and bleeding
a weaver-bird is tangerine the harpy is past
                 caring
the condor likewise in his mangy boa
they stare out across monkey-hill the elephants
Ireland
the light creeps down their old home canyon
sucks me aloof to that old reliable
the burning btm of George the drill
ah across the way a adder
broaches her rat
white as snow
in her dazzling oven strom of peristalsis
limae labor

ah father father that art in heaven

I find me taking the Crystal Palace
for the Blessed Isles from Primrose Hill
alas I must be that kind of person
hence in Ken Wood who shall find me
my breath held in the midst of thickets
none but the most quarried lovers

I surprise me moved by the many a funnel
                    hinged
for the obeisance to Tower Bridge
the viper's curtsy to and from the City
till in the dusk a lighter
blind with pride
tosses aside the scarf of the bascules
then in the grey hold of the ambulance
throbbing on the brink ebb of sighs
then I hug me below among the canaille
until a guttersnipe blast his cernèd eyes
demanding 'ave I done with the Mirror
I stump off in a fearful rage under Married
                    Men's Quarters
Bloody Tower
and afar off at all speed screw me up Wren's
                    giant bully
and curse the day caged panting on the platform
under the flaring urn
I was not born Defoe

but in Ken Wood
who shall find me

(36)

my brother the fly
the common housefly
sidling out of darkness into light
fastens on his place in the sun
whets his six legs
revels in his planes his poisers
it is the autumn of his life
he could not serve typhoid and mammon

Serena II

this clonic earth

see-saw she is blurred in sleep
she is fat half dead the rest is free-wheeling
part the black shag the pelt
is ashen woad
snarl and howl in the wood wake all the birds
hound the harlots out of the ferns
this damfool twilight threshing in the brake
bleating to be bloodied
this crapulent hush
tear its heart out

in her dreams she trembles again
way back in the dark old days panting
in the claws of the Pins in the stress of her hour
the bag writhes she thinks she is dying
the light fails it is time to lie down
Clew Bay vat of xanthic flowers
Croagh Patrick waned Hindu to spite a pilgrim
she is ready she has laid down above all the
                    islands of glory
straining now this Sabbath evening of garlands
with a yo-heave-ho of able-bodied swans
out from the doomed land their reefs of tresses

in a hag she drops her young
the whales in Blacksod Bay are dancing
the asphodels come running the flags after
she thinks she is dying she is ashamed

she took me up on to a watershed
whence like the rubrics of a childhood
behold Meath shining through a chink in the
                    hills
posses of larches there is no going back on
a rout of tracks and streams fleeing to the sea
kindergartens of steeples and then the harbour
like a woman making to cover her breasts
and left me

with whatever trust of panic we went out
with so much shall we return
there shall be no loss of panic between a man
                    and his dog
bitch though he be

sodden packet of Churchman
muzzling the cairn
it is worse than dream
the light randy slut can't be easy
this clonic earth
all these phantoms shuddering out of focus
it is useless to close the eyes
all the chords of the earth broken like a woman
                    pianist's

the toads abroad again on their rounds
sidling up to their snares
the fairy-tales of Meath ended
so say your prayers now and go to bed
your prayers before the lamps start to sing
                behind the larches
here at these knees of stone
then to bye-bye on the bones

Serena III

fix this pothook of beauty on this palette
you never know it might be final

or leave her she is paradise and then
plush hymens on your eyeballs

or on Butt Bridge blush for shame
the mixed declension of those mammae
cock up thy moon thine and thine only
up up up to the star of evening
swoon upon the arch-gasometer
on Misery Hill brand-new carnation
swoon upon the little purple
house of prayer
something heart of Mary
the Bull and Pool Beg that will never meet
not in this world

whereas dart away through the cavorting scapes
bucket o'er Victoria Bridge that's the idea
slow down slink down the Ringsend Road
Irishtown Sandymount puzzle find the Hell
        Fire
the Merrion Flats scored with a thrillion sigmas

Jesus Christ Son of God Saviour His Finger
girls taken strippin that's the idea
on the Bootersgrad breakwind and water
the tide making the dun gulls in a panic
the sands quicken in your hot heart
hide yourself not in the Rock keep on the move
keep on the move

Malacoda

thrice he came
the undertaker's man
impassible behind his scutal bowler
to measure
is he not paid to measure
this incorruptible in the vestibule
this malebranca knee-deep in the lilies
Malacoda knee-deep in the lilies
Malacoda for all the expert awe
that felts his perineum mutes his signal
sighing up through the heavy air
must it be it must be it must be
find the weeds engage them in the garden
hear she may see she need not

to coffin
with assistant ungulata
find the weeds engage their attention
hear she must see she need not

to cover
to be sure cover cover all over
your targe allow me hold your sulphur
divine dogday glass set fair

stay Scarmilion stay stay
lay this Huysum on the box
mind the imago it is he
hear she must see she must
all aboard all souls
half-mast aye aye

nay

Da Tagte Es

redeem the surrogate goodbyes
the sheet astream in your hand
who have no more for the land
and the glass unmisted above your eyes

Echo's Bones

asylum under my tread all this day
their muffled revels as the flesh falls
breaking without fear or favour wind
the gantelope of sense and nonsense run
taken by the maggots for what they are

1935

III Two Poems

I. Cascando

1.

why not merely the despaired of
occasion of
wordshed

is it not better abort than be barren

the hours after you are gone are so leaden
they will always start dragging too soon
the grapples clawing blindly the bed of want
bringing up the bones the old loves
sockets filled once with eyes like yours
all always is it better too soon than never
the black want splashing their faces
saying again nine days never floated the loved
nor nine months
nor nine lives

2.

saying again
if you do not teach me I shall not learn

saying again there is a last
even of last times
last times of begging
last times of loving
of knowing not knowing pretending
a last even of last times of saying
if you do not love me I shall not be loved
if I do not love you I shall not love

the churn of stale words in the heart again
love love love thud of the old plunger
pestling the unalterable
whey of words

terrified again
of not loving
of loving and not you
of being loved and not by you
of knowing not knowing pretending
pretending

I and all the others that will love you
if they love you

3.

unless they love you

1936

ier reflux

uis les pas
   lumières

1937

2. Saint-Lô

Vire will wind in other shadows
unborn through the bright ways tremble
and the old mind ghost-forsaken
sink into its havoc

1946

1. Dieppe

encore le der
le galet mort
le demi-tour
vers les vieill

2.

my way is in the sand flowing
between the shingle and the dune
the summer rain rains on my life
on me my life harrying fleeing
to its beginning to its end

my peace is there in the receding mist
when I may cease from treading these long
        shifting thresholds
and live the space of a door
that opens and shuts

3.

que ferais-je sans ce monde sans visage sans
                questions
où être ne dure qu'un instant où chaque instant
verse dans le vide dans l'oubli d'avoir été
sans cette onde où à la fin
corps et ombre ensemble s'engloutissent
que ferais-je sans ce silence gouffre des mur-
                mures
haletant furieux vers le secours vers l'amour
sans ce ciel qui s'élève
sur la poussière de ses lests

que ferais-je je ferais comme hier comme
                aujourd'hui
regardant par mon hublot si je ne suis pas seul
à errer et à virer loin de toute vie
dans un espace pantin
sans voix parmi les voix
enfermées avec moi

1948

3.

what would I do without this world faceless
               incurious
where to be lasts but an instant where every
               instant
spills in the void the ignorance of having been
without this wave where in the end
body and shadow together are engulfed
what would I do without this silence where the
               murmurs die
the pantings the frenzies towards succour
               towards love
without this sky that soars
above its ballast dust

what would I do what I did yesterday and the
               day before
peering out of my deadlight looking for another
wandering like me eddying far from all the
               living
in a convulsive space
among the voices voiceless
that throng my hiddenness

4.

je voudrais que mon amour meure
qu'il pleuve sur le cimetière
et les ruelles où je vais
pleurant celle qui crut m'aimer

1948

4.

I would like my love to die
and the rain to be falling on the graveyard
and on me walking the streets
mourning the first and last to love me

(translated from the French
by the author)